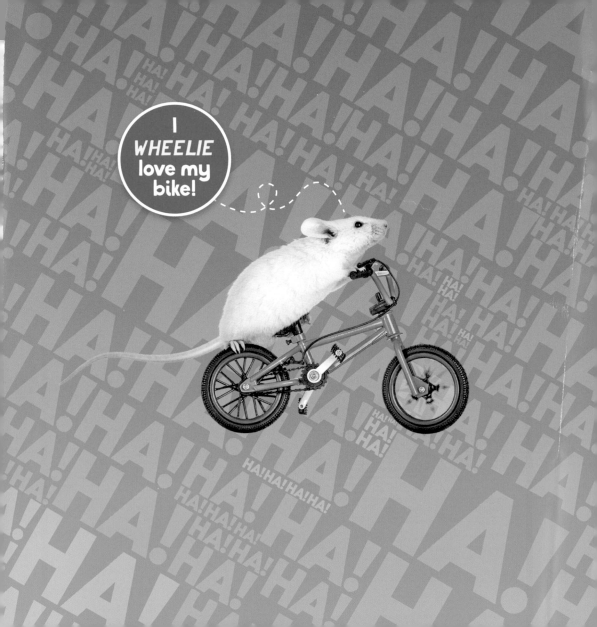

Just Joking

FUNNY

Animals 2

CRITTER COMEDIANS,

PUNNY PETS, and

HILARIOUS HIJINKS

There are
TOUCAN-DLES
on my
cake!

NATIONAL
GEOGRAPHIC
KiDS

NATIONAL GEOGRAPHIC
WASHINGTON, D.C.

Whose used **shoes** did Sue's dog **chew?**

The Angry Birds game was downloaded **500 MILLION TIMES** in just two years!

Angry Bird buddies Chuck, Red, and Bomb pose for a picture.

In the second Angry Birds movie, sworn enemies (pigs and birds) must fight **TOGETHER** against a new threat.

6

CRITTER
COMEDIANS
Angry Birds

WHAT DO YOU CALL A BIRD THAT CAN'T FLY? OK, yes, a penguin—but that's not who we're talking about. These particular flightless fowls are also famous for feeling a little bit ... angry. In fact, you might call them angry birds!

Unlike most birds, the Angry Bird flock can't fly. But that's only one reason they're so furious. The real cause? A group of no-good, green, greedy pigs who keep stealing the birds' eggs! These pigs are hungry for breakfast, and eggs are on the menu (hold the bacon). What's a bird to do? Save the eggs, of course!

Led by the angriest bird, Red, these feathered friends are on a mission to save their eggs and stop the pigs once and for all. Angry Birds launched themselves onto the scene with a game that has been downloaded over three billion times, and have since starred in two movies. One thing's for certain: No matter *how* angry they get, these birds of a feather always stick together!

You've **GOAT** a friend in me!

9

There are more than **1 BILLION** cattle in the world.

BOVINE
B·E·S·T·I·E·S

THINK OF WHERE YOU MET YOUR BEST FRIEND. Was it at the playground? Was it at school? Or maybe it was at camp? Well, if you happen to be a cow, chances are you'll meet your best friend in the barnyard.

Researchers have found that most cows, like people, have BFFs. Not only do these bovine besties love hanging out, but their *mooo*-ds seem to improve when they're together, too! To prove this, researchers penned two cows that didn't know each other together for 30 minutes and tracked their heart rates. They then repeated this test with two cattle comrades and found the results *udder*-ly shocking. When the cattle pals were together, their heart rates were lower and they were less stressed.

It also appears that barnyard buddies are smarter when they are together! Another research study found that chummy cows were better at problem-solving than cows that were paired with a partner they didn't hang around with. It just goes to show—the power of friendship is un-*bull*-ievable!

Some cows produce **MORE MILK** while listening to music or watching TV.

BE FRIE

We met in the **CALF-ETERIA!**

ST NDS

Now that's what I call **FAST FOOD!**

13

My instructor says my flying is just *PLANE* awesome!

LESTER WAS **ALL EARS** IN PILOT SCHOOL AND **FLEW** TO THE **TOP** OF HIS CLASS.

ANIMAL:

Chicken

NAME:

Sheriff Beakman

FAVORITE PASTIME:

Yolking around

FAVORITE SAYING:

"I suspect *fowl* play."

You're *HISSSS-TERICAL!* And so smart.

ERNIE WAS A REAL **SNAKE CHARMER.**

17

Stray Cat Inherits Estate

YOU COULD CALL THIS A CLASSIC RAGS-TO-RICHES *TAIL!*
Tommaso was a stray cat living on the streets of Rome, Italy, until he was taken in by a wealthy property owner. His new owner, Maria Assunta, was a 94-year-old widow and a *paw*-shionate cat lover. In fact, Maria was so in-*cat*-uated with Tommaso that she wanted to make sure he would be taken care of after she passed on.

Since animals can't legally inherit directly, Maria entrusted a person close to her with the task of managing Tommaso's fortune, houses, and well-being. Soon, Tommaso was not only no longer a stray, but was worth the equivalent of a cool $13 million—*no mitten!*

In addition to money, he also inherited some valuable ar-*cat*-tecture in the form of multiple apartments and houses all over Italy.

Now Tommaso is *feline* fine while living the sweet life with his guardian in the Roman countryside. Not too shabby for a cat from the streets!

A
GERMAN SHEPHERD
named Gunther was left
$80 MILLION
in his owner's will.

Gigoo, a
BRITISH CHICKEN,
inherited
$15 MILLION.
That's quite a nest egg!

Tommaso is a cat like the one shown here.

19

ANIMAL:

Dromedary camel

NAME:

Hyde

FAVORITE GAME:

Hide-and-seek

FAVORITE SAYING:

"You can't see me,

I'm *camel*-flaged!"

Venus's social media tagline is "0% photoshopped, 100% born this way!"

CRITTER
COMEDIANS

Venus the Two-Faced Cat

VENUS the model certainly knows how to command a *cat*walk. That's because anywhere she walks is a catwalk for Venus the cat! Venus is a model feline—and a feline model—who poses with *cat*-titude on social media and me-*wows* legions of fans. But Venus isn't just a celeb-*kitty*—she also promotes good causes, such as animal adoption and welfare.

Venus was a homeless stray abandoned on a North Carolina, U.S.A., dairy farm before she caught the eye of her human family. This tortoiseshell kitty was born with a rare but beautiful face that is exactly half black and half orange. She also has one green eye and one blue eye. Happily, Venus was adopted and given a home. Her new family soon discovered their feline's striking good looks and playful *cat*-titude made her a natural in front of the camera. Venus has scratched up an impressive 4.5 million social media followers who like nothing more than to admire her, see her dress up in silly costumes (Halloween cat-witch, anyone?), and hang—upside down—with her feline family.

Venus is thought to be a **CHIMERA,** which is an animal whose cells contain **TWO DIFFERENT** sets of DNA.

Venus sure knows how to capitalize on her *claw*-some looks!

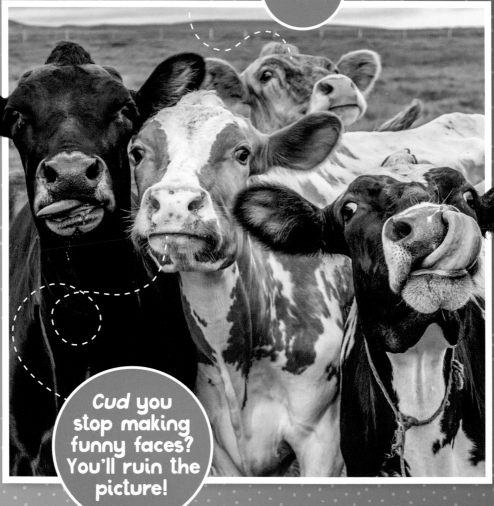

24

Six sickly
stick insects.

MOVES LIKE
SPARKLEMUFFIN

YOU MAY NEVER HAVE THOUGHT of an arachnid as a dance icon, but that might be because you've never come across a peacock spider.

Peacock spiders are tiny jumping spiders, measuring around .25 inch (6 mm) long—but what they lack in size they make up for in style! To attract mates, male peacock spiders are known to unleash some dance moves that would leave even the most famous of pop stars green with envy. They start by raising their back set of legs up in the air, and then scurry to and fro while shaking, rolling, and bopping. These slick moves aren't just for show, though—all that shaking creates a vibration that female peacock spiders can sense.

And, of course, as any dancer knows, awesome moves need great outfits to go with them. One type of peacock spider, known as Sparklemuffin, sports vibrant red and blue stripes on its midsection. Another, nicknamed Skeletorus, has striking black and white stripes. Skilled and stylish?

Dance on, peacock spiders!

JUMPING SPIDERS hunt their prey instead of weaving webs.

I've got **FOUR** *left* feet!

More than **20 NEW** species of **PEACOCK SPIDERS** have been discovered in the last few years.

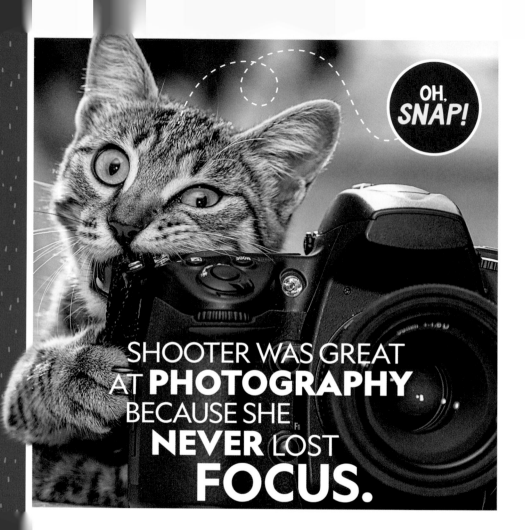

What kind of movies do cows like?

BULL-ockbusters?

That's *UDDER*-ly ridiculous—the answer is *MOO*-sicals.

Giraffe and Ostrich Are BFFs

WHAT DO YOU GET IF YOU CROSS an ostrich and a giraffe? You get the best of friends!

Wilma the ostrich and Bea the giraffe met at the Busch Gardens Tampa Bay theme park in Florida, U.S.A. There, in the park's 65-acre (26-ha) Serengeti Plain exhibit, they live among other African animals such as zebras, elephants, and rhinos. While most animals will usually pal around with their own species, zookeepers noticed that Wilma and Bea did no such thing. Instead, the unlikely pair had become inseparable.

Sure, the two have some things in common: They are both herbivores and both come from the same geographical region of Africa. But that doesn't explain why this odd couple has formed such a strong connection. Maybe the long-necked beauties share an affection for scarves, or perhaps they both love to stretch their lanky legs. Whatever the reason, zookeepers say that despite ample space to roam, Wilma and Bea still choose to spend all of their time together. Squad goals!

Bea frequently **LICKS** Wilma's face with her long tongue.

I think I need a breath mint.

Female giraffes are around **15 FEET (4.6 M) TALL,** while female ostriches can reach about **6.5 FEET (2 M) TALL.**

31

BOOP!
Got your
nose.

32

33

Goats Guzzle Grass

RUNNING BEHIND ON YOUR CHORES? Can't bribe your little sister to cut the grass for you? Here's a solution: Hire a goat to do it! No, we aren't *kid*ding around. Companies in the United States and Canada have started renting herds of goats as an environmentally friendly alternative to landscaping.

In addition to being adorable, a gang of hungry goats will save on electricity and gas used to power heavy equipment. They are also very light-footed and can work in rough terrain where mowers and saws can't reach. And as a bonus, goats will typically eat the "problem" vegetation, such as poison ivy, without tearing through prized grasses and plants.

To begin the goat mowing, the companies set up temporary fencing around the designated areas. Then they bring in the goats and let them do their stuff. The only thing left behind when they are done is ... ahem ... *fertilizer,* and even that helps the newly trimmed vegetation grow again.

And did we mention? It's adorable!

Have you *GOAT* any salad dressing?

Goats can be taught their name and to **COME WHEN CALLED** like a dog.

In some places, you can take a **YOGA CLASS** with a goat.

They weren't ready for a **CAT BURGLAR!**

ANIMAL:

Mouse

NAME:

Speedy

FAVORITE JOB:

Competitive biker

FAVORITE SAYING:

"I *wheelie* love riding my bike!"

UNDERSEA CHRISTMAS TREES

WHEN YOU HEAR "CHRISTMAS TREE WORMS," what comes to mind—images of pine-eating invaders? Well, rest assured: Christmas tree worms are actually common marine worms, and they neither dine on nor live in Christmas trees. So why the wacky name? One reason: their festive appearance!

The worms' tube-shaped bodies are topped by two feathery crowns that resemble small, colorful Christmas trees. These "trees" allow the worms to breathe, and to catch tasty dinners of microscopic plants and phytoplankton. Christmas tree worms—unlike most actual Christmas trees—can be found living on tropical coral reefs around the world. And unlike the real deal, these "trees" are quite small, measuring around 1.5 inches (3.8 cm) in length.

And would you believe that these *tree*-mendous creatures are one of the most widely recognized marine worms in the world? Their beautiful, vibrantly colored trees can be easily spotted and identified by divers ... or by any passing sleigh and reindeer. Now if we could just find a tiny little star to put on top of each of them!

The feathery structures of the crowns are both

STICKY
AND
SPIKY.

A Christmas tree worm can live **10 to 20 YEARS.**

Hey! Quit **HORSING** AROUND!

BEAK- a-boo!

41

Herman was born with larger-than-life eyeballs, but don't worry—his condition doesn't hurt him.

42

Cats can't see in the dark, but they can see in **VERY LOW LIGHT.**

CRITTER COMEDIANS

Herman the Scaredy-Cat

FEAST YOUR EYES ON Herman the scaredy-cat! All right, so he may not actually be scared, but his extra-large eyes give him a look of constant surprise. Hermie, as he is affectionately called, is an exotic shorthair cat from Copenhagen, Denmark. He was born with larger than normal eyeballs, which give him his adorably funny, eye-popping expression.

His owner, Shirley, needs to keep her eyes peeled for mischief. Herman has a fondness for footwear and can be found playing with his favorite shoelace or batting around one of Shirley's shoes. It's a habit that once led to Herman getting his head stuck in a sneaker until he was freed by his human. He never made that mistake again! When it's time for a little shut-eye, Herman does the opposite. His oversize orbs cause him to sleep with his eyes partially open. Even so, you can always tell when he's snoozing—his loud (and adorable) snoring is a telltale sign.

The only thing bigger than Herman's eyes is his heart. He is known for his loving temperament and for demanding attention with a meow and a tap of the paw ... and that's something Herman's nonfeline friends and fans are happy to give.

Cats have **VERTICAL PUPILS,** which change shape faster than round ones.

43

Willy went **west** to watch **walruses.**

WALRUS SPOTTING

TIME FOR POPCORN!

WHO LOVES POPCORN? If you answered "guinea pigs," you are totally correct. But not the edible, delicious kind of popcorn—rather than a salty snack, this kind of popcorn is a sweet guinea pig move! An excited guinea pig will often jump, twist, and hop wildly in the air during excited bursts of energy. Popcorning pigs can jump while they are running or from a complete standstill. They often even let out excited little squeaks.

While the scientific term for these jumps is "pronking," guinea pig owners prefer the term "popcorning." Why? Well ... because it's way cuter! The name also fits because of how suddenly the hops can happen, much like a kernel of corn will pop. This behavior happens in healthy guinea pigs young and old, so if you see it in action, you can be assured that your little piggy is happy, fit, and ... adorable.

Happy guinea pigs and hungry humans can agree: Popcorn is the best!

RABBITS make a similar move, but it is called **"BINKYING."**

Guinea pigs are not actually part of the **PIG FAMILY.**

These low ceilings are *GIRAFFING* me crazy!

49

Judy is the **FIRST RABBIT** on Zootopia's police force.

Judy flashes her badge while Nick flashes his smile.

JUST ZOO IT.

lemmings

OFFICER
TRUST
SECURITY BADGE
POLICE

CRITTER COMEDIANS
Nick Wilde and Judy Hopps

WHAT DO YOU GET WHEN YOU COMBINE a streetwise, funny fox with a *hop*-timistic bunny? A hilarious crime-fighting duo from the movie *Zootopia*!

Nick Wilde has all the traits of a clever fox. He's quick with the one-liners and even faster on his feet. He's been around the block in the big animal city of Zootopia and is a bit of a con man—er, con fox. Nick is always looking for a way to make a quick buck, like the time he tricked a police officer into buying him a huge lollipop which he then melted down into smaller lollipops and sold to unwitting customers. Of course, it just so happened that police officer was Judy Hopps ... oops!

Luckily for Nick, quick-thinking and determined Judy offered Nick a second chance if he agreed to help her solve her first crime. And even though Judy is continually frustrated by Nick's im-*paw*-sible antics, the hilarious duo always manages to save the day.

Nick Wilde wanted to be a member of the Zootopia **JUNIOR RANGERS** when he was young.

51

ANIMAL:

French bulldog

NAME:

Frank

FAVORITE HANGOUT:

Backyard BBQs

FAVORITE SAYING:

"I always try to blend in at parties!"

The sneering **deer** is really Weary.

SPIKE'S PARTY DECORATIONS ARE ALWAYS
ON POINT.

My party hat is looking *SHARP!*

Where do snakes kiss at Christmas time?

YULE have to tell me.

Under the HISS-LETOE.

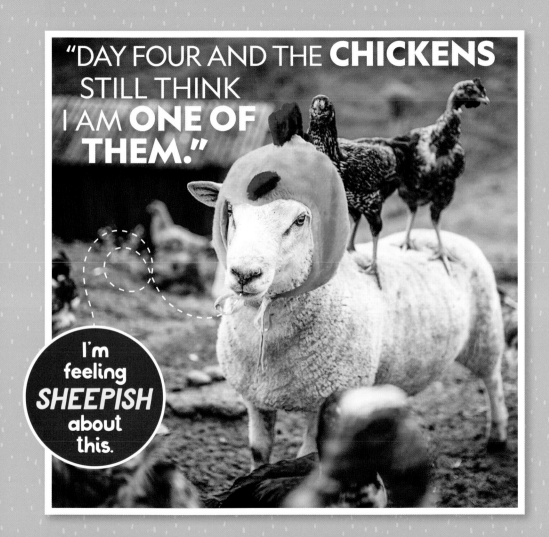

Unicorn Causes Police Chase

HAVE YOU HEARD ABOUT THE UNICORN that led cops on a three-hour chase? OK, so maybe it wasn't an actual unicorn … it was a pony dressed like one! Juliet is a 400-pound (181-kg) Shetland pony from California, U.S.A. Her owner often dresses her up as a unicorn for photo shoots and birthday parties, but at one particular birthday bash, Juliet decided to hoof it.

Not one to stall, the perky pony managed to escape the birthday party and went on a magical adventure. She was spotted *foaling* around on California roadways. The Highway Patrol was alerted that a unicorn was wandering the streets and so began a three-hour chase. Authorities were having such a hard time wrangling her that they eventually called in a helicopter to help track the fantastical fugitive. Still, Juliet could not be roped in and managed to evade capture. Finally, as a last resort, Juliet's owner enlisted the help of Shady—a neighboring horse who happened to be Juliet's best friend. When Juliet saw Shady, she followed her bestie into a trailer, and the *uni-corny* chase finally came to an end.

As a "punishment" for her crime, Juliet's owners took away her unicorn horn and made her wear devil horns for the day.

I am a naughty pony! For all the trouble I caused last night, they took away my unicorn horn and gave me these horns instead.

I'm a pony on the run!

Shetland ponies can pull **TWICE** their own weight.

Shetland ponies come from the **SHETLAND ISLANDS** in the northern part of Scotland.

Wily weasels weathered wetter weather better.

CRITTER
COMEDIANS
Jiffpom

WHO WEIGHS FIVE POUNDS (2.3 kg), holds two world records, and has his own mobile phone app? Jiffpom—that's who!

This precious Pomeranian pooch lives in Los Angeles amidst the celebrities, but he's also a star in his own right: Jiffpom is the fastest dog on two legs. That's right: two legs. Jiff is swift on both his front and hind paws. He holds the world record for running 33 feet (10 m) on his hind legs in just 6.56 seconds and 16 feet (4.9 m) on his front paws in 7.76 seconds. In addition to being a speed master, Jiffpom also has other skills. He can ride a skateboard, shake a paw, and bow to his subjects ... that is, his fans. And boy, does this good boy have fans: He has 26 million social media followers!

Jiff's fame has brought him awards (including the 2018 Nickelodeon's Kids' Choice for favorite social media pet), fame (as a model and celebrity), and fortune. It's not known exactly how much this hard-working "floof" is worth, but it is a safe bet this supercutie isn't hard up for kibble.

Despite only weighing less than 10 pounds (4.5 kg), Pomeranians are descended from **SLED DOGS.**

Mozart once dedicated a **MUSICAL PIECE** to his Pomeranian.

Jiffpom has more than 26 million social media followers.

Oh, **CUB ON!** How do I get down?

BRUIN REALIZED HE HAD MADE AN **EM-*BEAR*-RASSING** MISTAKE.

Proportionally, a crow's brain is **BIGGER** than a human's brain.

BIRD GENIUSES

HAVE YOU EVER SEEN A CROW with a calculator? Or how about a bird poring over some science books? You might not suspect it just by looking at them, but crows are no birdbrains. In fact, the feathery fowls might just be the Einsteins of the avian world.

Some researchers think that crows are as smart as apes and young children. Does this mean that crows will soon be taking classes at your local colleges? Maybe not, but it does mean that these brainy birds can count, use tools, recognize faces, and even change their "accents." For example, when a crow joins another flock—or "murder," as they're called—it often changes the way it caws and squawks to fit in. Other clever crows have been observed placing nuts in crosswalks and waiting for cars to crack them, showing that the birds can even understand traffic lights.

It seems that being a birdbrain is actually something to crow about!

Crows have caused **BLACK-OUTS** in Japan by stealing cables to build their nests.

Does anyone know where my library card is?

AMUSING
ANIMALS

ANIMAL:

Cat

NAME:

Herb

FAVORITE FOOD:

Anything but vegetables

FAVORITE SAYING:

"I *yam not* a fan."

Hey! Let us have a turn!

Sheldon, you are being *SHELL*-fish with the ball!

SNEEZING MONKEY

Anyone got a hankie?

AAH, THE SOUNDS OF A MOUNTAIN FOREST—a babbling brook, the calls of the birds, and ... sneezing?

That sneezing sound floating on the mountain air comes from the Myanmar snub-nosed monkey, also known as the sneezing monkey. Discovered in the Himalayan mountains in 2011, the sneezing monkey is known for its peculiarly shaped schnoz. However, because of its unique shape, a sneezing monkey's nose poses a problem in the rainy climate of Southeast Asia. Whenever it rains, the drops fall right into the monkeys' nostrils, causing them to go bananas with sneezing!

The locals say it is easy to find the monkeys in the wild because they can be heard sneezing from up in the trees. In fact, it takes a lot of monkeying around for them not to sneeze—they have to keep their heads between their knees when the rain starts. Talk about monkey business! These cuties could definitely use an umbrella and a pack of tissues.

Their hands are covered in such thick hair, it looks like they are **WEARING MITTENS.**

Although it was only recently discovered, the sneezing monkey is **CRITICALLY ENDANGERED,** with only around 400 left in the wild.

COLD MEDICINE

I love *HORSING AROUND.*

I look pretty *FLY* in this outfit!

WAFTING WHALE WASTE

WHAT HAS A GIANT HEAD AND POOPS GOLD? The sperm whale, of course! OK, so maybe it doesn't poop gold, but what it does "deposit" into the ocean—called ambergris—is one of the world's strangest natural occurrences and has been described for over a thousand years as "treasure of the sea."

Ambergris is a waxlike substance that comes from sperm whales. It forms in a whale's intestines and helps protect the whale's inner organs from sharp objects such as squid beaks. Scientists once thought that ambergris was ejected from a whale's mouth, but they now believe that it comes out of the ... er ... other end. The ambergris then hardens as it bobs along in the ocean. As the ambergris dries out, it produces a *fin*-tastic smell that has made it much prized by perfume makers. Seriously, a pound (.45 kg) of the stuff once sold for $63,000. That's a whale of a price for waste!

Anyone know where the little whale's room is?

Sperm whales can go **90 MINUTES** between breaths and **DIVE DOWN** more than 3,280 feet (1,000 m).

Female sperm whales eat up to **800 SQUID** every day.

Dried ambergris is sometimes found washed up on shore.

Dream jobs for animals:

ALPACA-PELLA SINGER

SEAL ESTATE AGENT

DOG-UMENTARY FILMMAKER

DEER-DEVIL

FUR-TOGRAPHER

ANIMAL:

Chihuahua

NAME:

Claw-dia

FAVORITE DOG BREED:

Doberman *pincher*

FAVORITE SAYING:

"I'm not *shell*-fish!"

SAM WAS THE **WORST HUNTER** IN HIS **FAMILY.**

Where did that rat go??

Duck Lives Life of Luxury

WHO'S YOUR FAVORITE FAMOUS CANADIAN? Justin Bieber? Ryan Reynolds? Well, not for long! Without *feather* ado, this is your intro-*duck*-tion to Jeffery, a small-town celebrity living the high life. Of course, this Canadian is also a duck!

That's right—Jeffery is a duck. But unlike most farm animals, Jeffery is a full-*fledged* member of the household! He sleeps indoors (what, you think he'd sleep on just any nest?), chills out on the living room couch, and even has his own potty—a litter box!

Jeffery is well known in his part of town and, like any celebrity, enjoys a luxurious lifestyle. One day he's being chauffeured to the beach in his special car seat, and the next he's waddling through local stores, searching for his favorite snacks. This dashing duck even has his own fancy duds—a bumblebee costume! And even more luxuriously, Jeffery has a custom swimming pool where he enjoys bathing, splashing, and swimming. This duck's life is definitely all it's *quacked* up to be!

I packed cheese and *quackers*.

Jeffery's favorite foods are worms, tomatoes, and **BANANA CHIPS.**

Jeffery often carries around a **STUFFED KITTY.**

87

TOAD–DAY is going to be un–FROG–getable!

SAM IS **ALWAY VERY** *HOP*-TIMISTIC.

Because of their **SHORT NOSES,** pugs are prone to colds.

Doug loves having his picture taken. When he sees a camera, his tail wags uncontrollably!

90

CRITTER COMEDIANS
Doug the Pug

WHO HAS A CURLY TAIL, a flat nose, a taste for the good life, and *pup*-peroni pizza? It's Doug the Pug, social media's king canine!

These days Doug pals around with rock stars and celebrities, but the perky pup wasn't always so popular. In fact, this superstar was once just a "regular" dog who spent his time snoozing on the couch and drooling over treats. But when his owner Leslie Mosier began posting Doug's mug on social media, a star was born—people went doggone crazy over Doug!

Doug is a natural ham, and he loves to pal around in goofy getups. From posing in France by the Eiffel Tower to starring in a music video, this doggy diva can't be stopped. Doug's fans are barking mad for his pooch pics and videos—they even line up to meet him! And that's not all: This popular pug has been nominated for several awards and has even published books. But don't worry, Doug hasn't let success go to his head—at the end of the day, he's still just a humble dog who loves a good nap on the couch.

A group of pugs is called a **GRUMBLE.**

ANIMAL:

Chicken

NAME:

Harry

FAVORITE HANGOUT:

The salon

FAVORITE SAYING:

"Can I *comb* over and visit?"

SUPERHERO
SALAMANDER

OK, SO IT CAN'T MAKE ITSELF INVISIBLE OR move as fast as a speeding bullet, but the Mexican axolotl (pronounced ACK-suh-LAH-tuhl) has a few superpowers that might make you jealous.

These powers? Oh, just measly super camouflage abilities. These rare salamanders can control the size of their pores to become lighter or darker and blend into their surroundings. And—oh, yeah—they can regenerate entire limbs or organs that have been damaged or cut off. If an axolotl loses a limb, the wound heals quickly and the animal begins to grow a new limb within days. Or if an axolotl needs a pair of lungs? No problem! It can just develop some! Born with an undeveloped set of lungs, this superhero salamander breathes underwater through the whisker-like gills on its head. If raised in the shallow end, this crafty amphibian can grow its own lungs to survive on land.

A camouflaged, lung-growing salamander that can regenerate its limbs? Nature beats any costumed crime-fighter, hands down!

AXOLOTLS
don't have
eyelids.

Axolotls were named after the ancient **AZTEC GOD** Xolotl.

It's a bird! It's a plane! No, it's SUPER AXOLOTL!

96

What kind of **COOKIES** do parrots eat?

Animal crackers?

MACAW-ROONS!

SUSIE DIDN'T KNOW THE **WORDS** TO THE **SONG.** SHE WAS JUST **WINGING** IT.

The black bat brought the black boot back.

Rat Eats Money in ATM

HAVE YOU EVER HEARD OF AN ALL-YOU-CAN-EAT ATM?
Well, maybe not, but a rat in India seems to have invented one!

When an ATM stopped dispensing cash in Tinsukia, India, technicians were called to the scene. They were completely surprised by what they found! A rat had crawled into the ATM through a tiny hole, squeezing past cables and wires, and made a home for itself. When the technicians opened the machine, they found the reason for the lack of cash: Most of the money inside had been shredded, and some of it had been eaten by the busy rat.

You gonna eat that?

The naughty nibbler munched and tore its way through 1.2 million rupees—equivalent to roughly $18,000 (US$)! The rupee-ripping rodent also made a nest out of the bills. Now that's a very swanky nest. It's still unknown whether the rat acted alone or is part of a tiny crime gang.

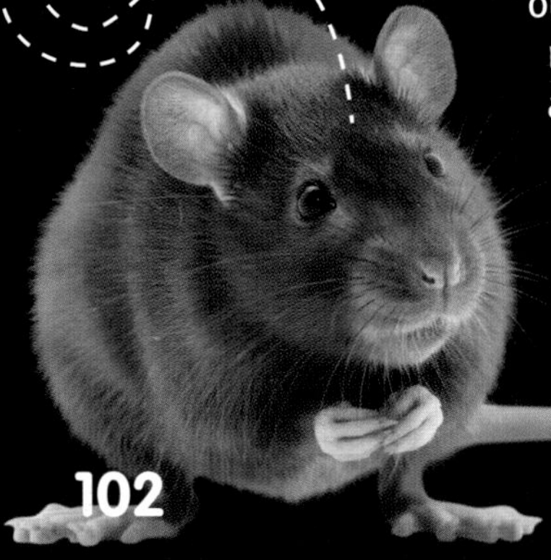

The guilty rat was one like those pictured here.

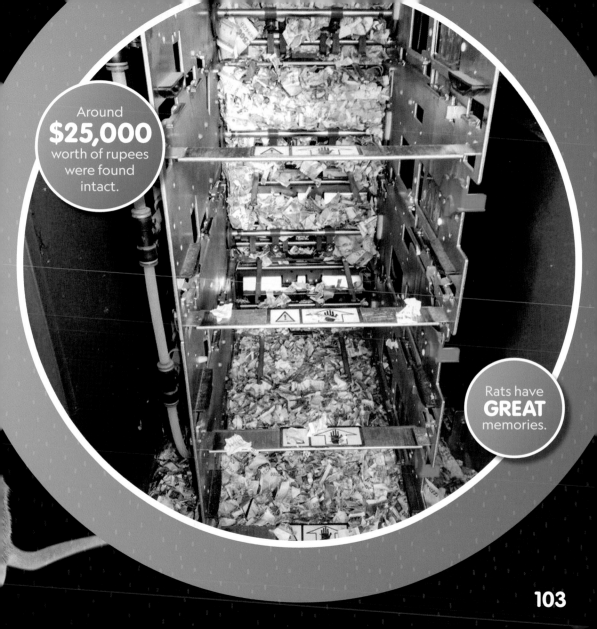

Around **$25,000** worth of rupees were found intact.

Rats have **GREAT** memories.

104

A day at the beach was an *EAR-*RESISTIBLE idea.

105

This Hello Kitty balloon made an appearance in the Macy's Thanksgiving Day Parade.

In Japan she is known as "KITTY-CHAN."

CRITTER COMEDIANS
Hello Kitty

GET READY, BECAUSE HELLO KITTY IS SET on world domination. OK, not really, but this catlike cutie sure has taken the planet by storm!

With whiskers, a soft, round face, a button nose, and *purr*-fect catlike ears, she might look like a pretty kitty, but the Hello Kitty character is actually a little girl. Born near London, England, Hello Kitty has since traveled around the world, making friends and gaining fans (though her best friend remains her twin sister, Mimmy). In fact, since her creation in 1974, Hello Kitty has slowly and steadily been taking over the world: She's become so popular that she's appeared in a cartoon series and in comics, and she has toys, clothes, games, theme parks, and more made in her likeness. She even recorded an album!

Despite her legions of fans, Hello Kitty isn't worried about fame. She much prefers to eat apple pie, play the piano, and hang out with her pet cat, Charmmy Kitty. But if she wanted to take over the world ... well, it might not be so bad!

Hello Kitty says she is **"FIVE APPLES TALL."**

107

AMUSING
ANIMALS

ANIMAL:

Guinea pig

NAME:

Hulk

FAVORITE FOOD:

Avo-*cardio*

FAVORITE SAYING:

"I can't *weight* to

get to the gym!"

I'm quite *FAWNED* of camouflage!

SECRET ASSASSIN!

An assassin bug paralyzing its prey

IT MIGHT SEEM LIKE JUST AN ORDINARY BUG, but the assassin bug is a master of disguise. And not just any disguise—a supercreepy one!

Acanthaspis petax, as it's scientifically known, feeds on ants. But first it has to catch them. How? By disguising itself as a mound of ants! This trickster bug injects saliva from its needle-like nose to paralyze its prey. It then sucks their organs dry and places their corpses on its sticky back. This disgusting—but effective—disguise makes the bug appear to be a moving group of ants. "Oh, look, some friends!" an unsuspecting ant might think. But no—it's a deadly assassin. Plus, this icky camouflage helps the assassin bug evade its own predators—spiders. Hey, it might sound gross, but it probably works much better than a fake mustache!

They call me **BUG.** James Bug.

An assassin bug has **STICKY PADS** on its front legs to help grip its prey.

Cockroaches
will die
**3 TO 4
SECONDS**
after an assassin
bug bite.

LLAMA go on a picnic tomorrow. Anyone want to come?

OWL pack a lunch.

IGUANA go now.

I think I'll **OTTER** another pizza ... wait, this isn't a cell phone.

CRITTER COMEDIANS
A hedgehog and her wiener dogs

Hedgehogs have about **5,000** spines.

INTERSPECIES FRIENDSHIP IS complicated. There's the language barrier for one thing. And will you like the same things? Fortunately, that's not a problem for Minnie, Maya, Stella, and Peanut. This foursome of hedgehog (Minnie) and dachshunds are best pals who never get prickly, even though the dogs have hunting and tunneling prey in their family history.

So, what makes them such a close group? For one thing, the stumpy-limbed dachshunds are not much taller than little Minnie. For another, they enjoy the same hobbies, such as begging for treats, scarfing down treats, and snoozing. Well, okay, Minnie doesn't beg. She's a sharp one, after all!

The quad squad are oddball family pets who live in England but have a social media fan base throughout the world. The wacky wieners often dress up like triplets, wearing pretty pink sweaters and silly floppy hats. No props and clothing for Minnie—she's happy to show off her impressive spines. They say the family that plays together stays together, and that's certainly true of this crew.

If they feel threatened, hedgehogs will curl up into a **PRICKLY BALL.**

Costumes at the animal Halloween party:

ZOM-BEES

RAM-PIRE

MIME-OCEROUS

DARTH GATOR

HIPSTER-POTAMUS

CRITTER
COMEDIANS

Punxsutawney Phil

FOR A GUY with only one job—on one day a year—Punxsutawney Phil sure gets a lot of attention. Each Groundhog Day, the world's most famous groundhog is called on to ... predict the weather!

Phil normally holes up for the winter in a cozy burrow in his hometown of Punxsutawney, Pennsylvania, U.S.A. Most days, he spends his time snoozing. But on February 2, he never fails to get up before dawn. That's because legend holds that if Phil sees his shadow on this day, it means six more weeks of winter. If there is no shadow, spring is said to be near! Phil (or some furry ancestor who looked just like him) has been "predicting" the length of winter in Pennsylvania since 1886. But the tradition of animals predicting the weather dates back many centuries. Are these predictions actually real? Probably not ... but either way, Phil is the toast of Punxsutawney!

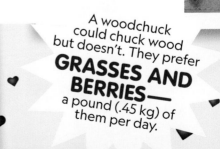

PUNXSUTAWNEY PHIL
PRESENTED
BY HIS ADMIRERS
JULY 9, 1977

A woodchuck could chuck wood but doesn't. They prefer **GRASSES AND BERRIES**— a pound (.45 kg) of them per day.

Punxsutawney Phil is held by his handler after making his annual prediction.

Groundhogs are also called **WOODCHUCKS.**

119

120

121

This Sea Lion Went to Market

CHECK YOUR SHOPPING LIST: BREAD, MILK, FISH, SEA LION?
At the Santa Cruz Fish Market in Puerto Ayora, in central Galápagos, Ecuador, you'll find all types of shoppers: tourists, locals, workers, as well as pelicans and sea lions!

That's right, these plucky pelicans and sneaky sea lions have discovered a shortcut to dinnertime. The fish market is located along the shore where these animals live and is stocked with all the mooching munchers' favorite fish: red snapper, grouper, and yellowfin tuna. So instead of hunting and fending for themselves in the ocean, these sneaky snackers waddle their way over and look for handouts. They are not disappointed.

The fish market has become a favorite of tourists who come for the delicious fish, but stay to watch the show as the sea life (and the occasional iguana) patiently wait to feast on tidbits the fishmongers throw their way.

Why hunt when you can belly your way up to the counter and place your order like everyone else?

A Galápagos sea lion can hold its breath for up to
20 MINUTES.

You gonna eat that?

In Spanish, Galápagos sea lions are called *lobos del mar*, which means **"WOLVES OF THE SEA."**

Can I get fries with that?

I'll take mine TO GO!

JAZZ
HANDS!

Bob brought
blue baboons.

FAINTING GOATS

Goats need their **HOOVES TRIMMED** regularly.

IF YOU'RE PLANNING A TRIP TO A HAUNTED HOUSE or a scary movie, it's probably best you leave your myotonic goat at home. They—quite literally—get scared stiff!

These adorably tiny goats are also called stiff-leg goats, wooden-leg goats, nervous goats, or fainting goats. However, they don't actually faint—instead, they fall over when they are startled, scared, or excited. That's because myotonic goats have a medical condition that causes their muscles to seize when they are frightened. But the stiffness only lasts for about 20 seconds, and it doesn't hurt the goats. Although it can cause them to fall over, as the animals get older they learn to lean against something to stay upright. And if you think this is going to slow them down, you've *goat another thing coming!*

Don't worry—the goats aren't harmed.

I don't have the **FAINTEST** idea why this happens!

Some **SCOTTISH TERRIERS** suffer from temporary paralysis if they get too excited.

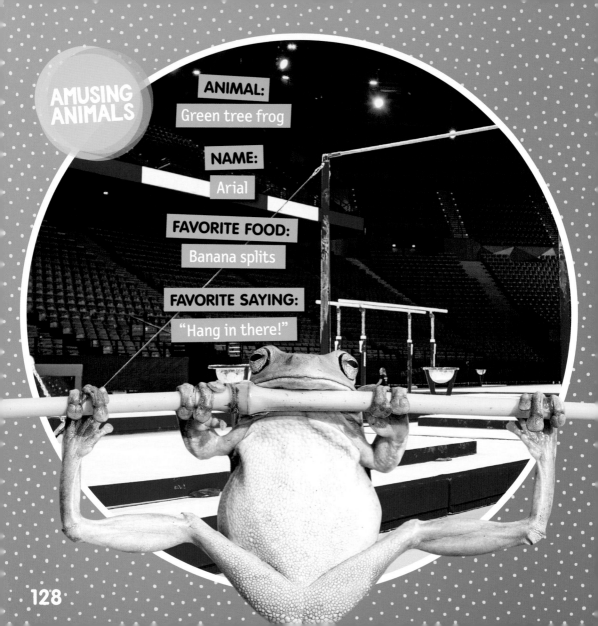

AMUSING ANIMALS

ANIMAL:
Green tree frog

NAME:
Arial

FAVORITE FOOD:
Banana splits

FAVORITE SAYING:
"Hang in there!"

I just caught a fish that was THIS BIG!

DOUG WAS KNOWN FOR **PUFFIN** UP HIS FISHING STORIES.

CRITTER COMEDIANS
Snoopy

WHAT KIND OF DOG SLEEPS ON *TOP* OF HIS DOGHOUSE? Well, the same kind of dog that dances on his hind legs, does magic tricks, and can ride a dirt bike.

His name is Snoopy and he's no ordinary pup. Originating in the "Peanuts" cartoon, Snoopy is the cartoon gang's loyal canine mascot. He is known for his wild fantasy life. Aside from being Charlie Brown's pet beagle, Snoopy has also fashioned several alter egos for himself. From a World War I flying ace to a world-famous disco dancer, and Blackbeagle the world-famous pirate to, well, a world-famous baseball manager, Snoopy does it all. That's doggone difficult for a four-legged fellow!

But even though he might not really be a pilot, a pirate, or a manager, Snoopy is a world-famous dog! He has even earned a star on the Hollywood Walk of Fame. So what does this world-renowned rover do when he isn't flying his doghouse like an airplane or finding a new profession to dominate? Snoopy is hounding the "Peanuts" gang with sloppy dog kisses.

Snoopy has been in the Macy's Thanksgiving Day Parade **39 TIMES**— more than any other balloon.

Snoopy has **SEVEN SIBLINGS:** Spike, Belle, Marbles, Olaf, Andy, Molly, and Rover.

Snoopy as the World War I Flying Ace, flying his doghouse into battle with his enemy, the Red Baron

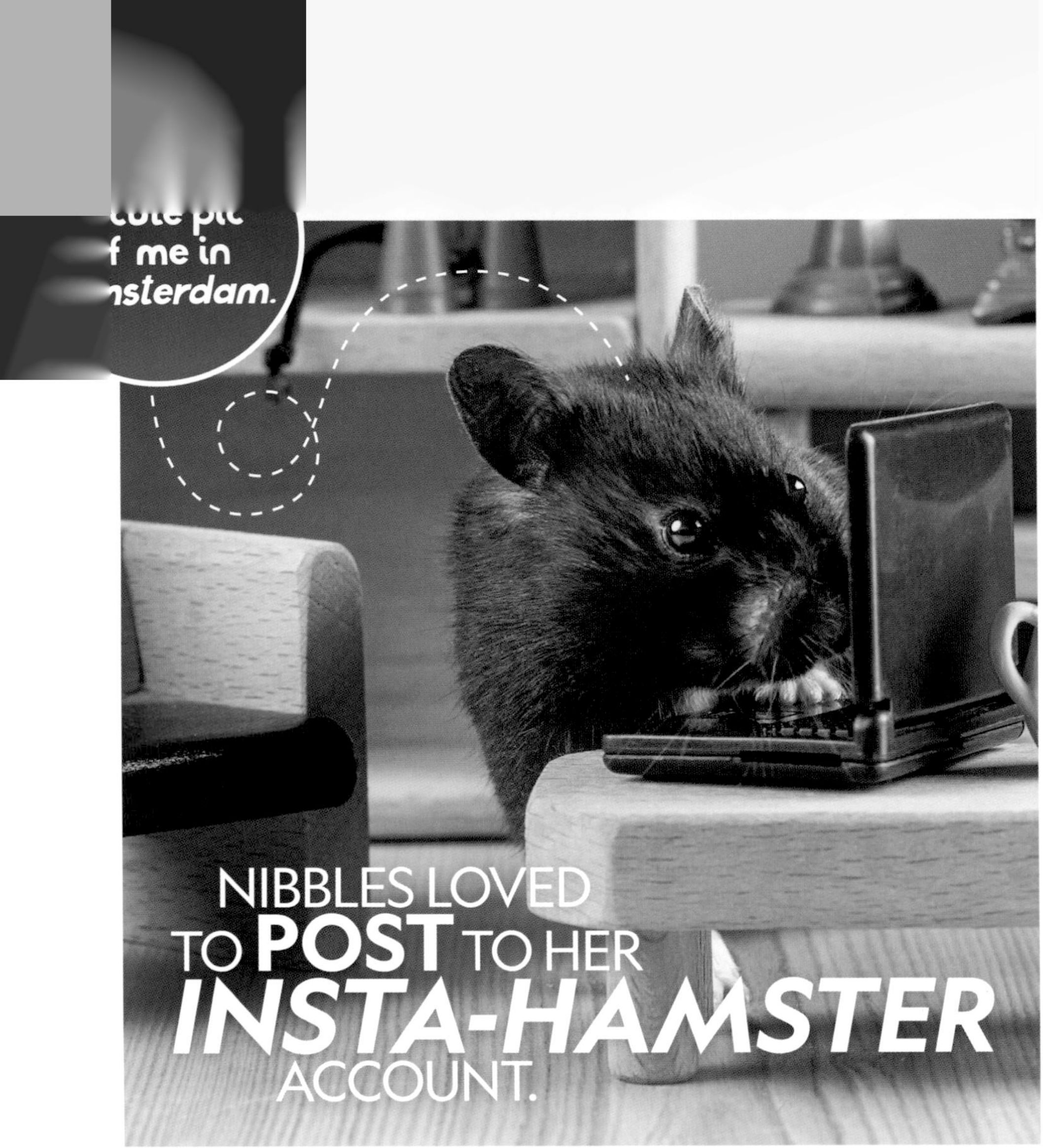

cute pic
of me in
msterdam.

NIBBLES LOVED
TO **POST** TO HER
INSTA-HAMSTER
ACCOUNT.

133

NINJA FROG

THE WORLD'S GREATEST DAD AWARD GOES TO ...
drumroll, please ... the reticulated glass frog!

Smaller than one inch (2.5 cm) long, this tiny frog is found in the rainforests of Costa Rica, Panama, Colombia, and Ecuador. But despite its size, the male is one tough amphibian!

When the female reticulated glass frog lays a clutch of eggs, she sticks them on a leaf. They are then entrusted to the male. And what better guardian than a father who has the skills of a ninja warrior? The male reticulated glass frog guards the clutch until they hatch. He has to watch them 24/7: The eggs are a favorite treat of the large and powerful rainforest wasp, which will stop at nothing to get those eggs. Nothing that is, except a kick in the head from Dad! Father Frog uses a series of ninja-like kicks to protect his young, and he will even wrestle other frogs who intrude on the territory.

Somebody get that frog a coffee mug that says "#1 Dad"!

When the
TADPOLES
hatch, they fall
off the leaves
to the water
below.

Reticulated glass frogs get their name from their completely **SEE-THROUGH BELLY SKIN.**

I get a **KICK** out of watching my kids!

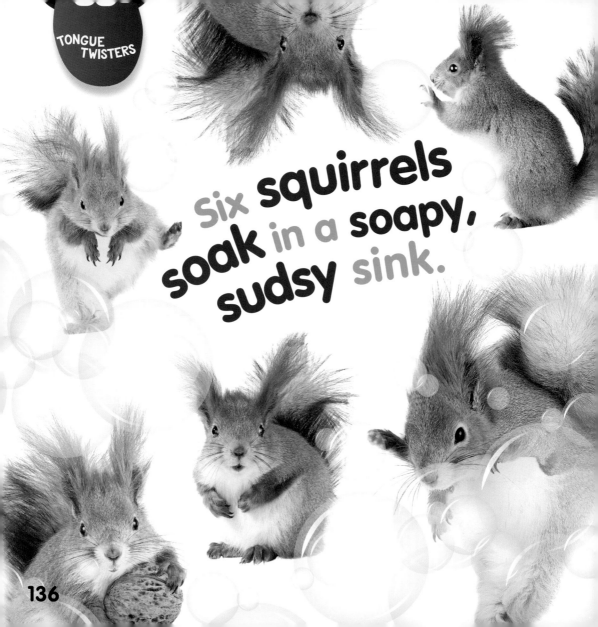

Six squirrels soak in a soapy, sudsy sink.

Can someone please let this CAT out of the bag?

BILL ALWAYS STAYED *CLAW-SITIVE* IN ANNOYING **SITUATIONS.**

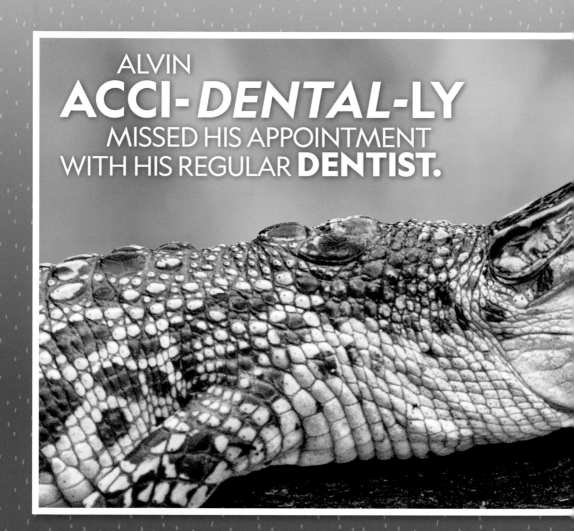

ALVIN
ACCI-*DENTAL*-LY
MISSED HIS APPOINTMENT
WITH HIS REGULAR **DENTIST.**

You need
to floss
more.

ANIMAL:

Rabbit

NAME:

Professor Warren

FAVORITE ACTIVITY:

Burrowing library books

FAVORITE SAYING:

"Don't worry, be *hoppy*."

Which animal serves in the **MILITARY?**

Is it wearing *CAMEL-*flage?

An *ARMY-*dillo.

ALPACAS produce 5 to 10 pounds (2.2 to 4.5 kg) of hair each year.

142

Llamas Attend Weddings

EVERYONE *LLOVES* A WEDDING: fancy clothes, tasty food, dancing, llamas—wait ... llamas? Yes, llamas! You *herd* it here first: A company in Oregon, U.S.A., will bring a pair of llamas or alpacas to your wedding event to make your special day even more *lla*-mazing. The llama or alpaca couple *wool* even arrive in their best wedding finery.

By day, the company's llamas and alpacas are used as therapy animals. They visit nursing homes, special-needs schools, and rehab facilities to bring smiles to people young and old. But by night, these helpful herbivores *alpaca* up their gear and hoof it on over to your wedding function.

Guests can pet, feed, and pose for pictures with the woolly wedding-goers, who arrive dressed to impress. Floral garlands (which can also double as a handy snack) or a dapper top hat and bow tie will help these four-legged friends blend in with the crowd and party *pasture* bedtime. Just don't expect any great dance moves ... llamas have two left feet!

Llama **DUNG** has been used as fuel.

143

Great gray goats graze green grassy groves.

... so I said to the zookeeper, "Gimme those bananas before I *GO APE!*"

CRITTER COMEDIANS
Donkey, Noble Steed

HE'S COOL, fearless (almost), and most definitely fast-talking. He's Donkey, or "Daunkeee," as Shrek calls him!

Best known for his role in the *Shrek* movies, Donkey met Shrek the Ogre when escaping from his owner. The two quickly became inseparable— much to Shrek's irritation! This is probably because of Donkey's habits, which could be described as, well, annoying. For one thing, he loves to talk ... a lot! In fact, the only times Donkey isn't talking are when he's singing at the top of his lungs. To Donkey, any time is a good time for a song—all day long, in the evening, before bed, in the middle of the night, in the early morning ... what, you don't want to be woken up by Donkey's braying? Too bad! When he wants to sing, Donkey's going to sing ... or at least hum. That's because (much like Shrek) Donkey is super stubborn—Shrek often has to trick his obstinate friend into doing things he doesn't want to do (even when they're for his own good!).

But underneath it all, Donkey is a true friend who sees people—and ogres—for who they really are. And when Donkey decides you are his friend, he'll bend over backward to help you out. Now that's worth singing about!

Donkey's appearance was based on a real **MINIATURE DONKEY** in California, U.S.A.

Donkey loves to eat **WAFFLES.**

Despite his look of irritation, Shrek is very fond of Donkey.

148

Quit **FOALING** around and get to work!

LENNY WAS **ALWAYS LYING DOWN** ON THE JOB.

I couldn't find my *hare*-brush.

HOPPER AND FLOPS WORE **HATS** ON BAD *HARE* DAYS.

ADITYA:

What can you find **HAUNTING** a chicken coop?

ASHWIN:

This sounds *peck*-uliar.

ADITYA:

A *POULTRY*-geist.

All that practice on the SCRATCHING POST has paid off!

MITTENS WAS **EXCITED** TO ACT AS **CAT-TAIN** OF THE **SHIP.**

Twelve tapirs twirled twelve twigs.

156

157

Chaser's **FAVORITE** toy is a bouncy blue ball.

I've got nothing to play with.

Dog Learns Language

FOR MOST DOGS, FAVORITE HOBBIES INCLUDE DIGGING HOLES, CHEWING SOCKS, rolling in stinky smells, and chasing their own tails. But Chaser the border collie seems to have loftier ambitions: She spends her time learning English!

When former psychology professor John Pilley first got Chaser, he knew that she was doggone smart. Curious to see how much the clever canine could learn, he began to teach her words by giving names to different dog toys. Chaser made an excellent student, and soon, her toy collection began to grow ... and so did her vocabulary! It wasn't long before Chaser knew more than 1,200 words. And not only was this fantastic Fido an A+ student, she also excelled at extra credit; Chaser even learned to tell the difference between verbs, adjectives, and nouns.

Chaser started to learn words at

TWO MONTHS OLD.

These days, Chaser lives with the Pilley family and continues practicing her favorite subject. Of course, even the best students can still get into mischief! When not kept busy, Chaser often sticks her nose into trouble ... but she's much too cute to ever earn a detention!

AMUSING ANIMALS

ANIMAL:
Polar bear

NAME:
Snoozer

FAVORITE TIME OF DAY:
Bedtime

FAVORITE SAYING:
"I can *bear*-ly stay awake!"

CRAIG FOUND AN **EASIER** WAY TO **GATHER FOOD** FOR WINTER.

This is *NUTS!*

BLUE TANGS are also called hippo tangs, blue surgeonfish, and doctor fish.

In addition to speaking whale, Dory can read "human English."

CRITTER
COMEDIANS
Dory the Fish

HI! HAVE YOU MET DORY? She's a blue tang fish with a sunny disposition and a penchant for making friends. Oh … you have met Dory? Well, she also has a bit of a memory problem!

First seen in the film *Finding Nemo,* Dory is famous for her short-term memory loss. Of course, she never lets that slow her down. Armed with her optimism, reading skills, and *fin*-tastic singing voice, Dory charms everyone she meets with her helpful nature and heart of gold. Most impressively, she helps Marlin the clownfish in the search for his missing son, Nemo. Sure, Dory often forgets Nemo's name and sometimes leads the group into dangerous situations (from hungry sharks to stinging jellyfish to the stomach of a whale), but she always sticks with her friends and manages to save the day.

Hi! Have you met Dory?

Dory
can speak
WHALE
(but not
very well).

EWAN:
Why did the police officer give the sheep a ticket?
LAMBERT:
Ewe must tell me.
EWAN:
Because he was a BAAAAAD driver.

This new phone is driving me *BANANAS!*

STEVE STARTED DOING HIS **MONKEY** **BUSINESS** ONLINE.

THIS CRAB IS (COCO)NUTs!

CLOSE YOUR EYES AND IMAGINE YOU'RE ON A BEAUTIFUL BEACH. The sun is shining, the water is calm, the sand is warm, and here comes a giant crab ... the size of a small dog?! No, you aren't dreaming—you're looking at a coconut crab.

This monster crab, found in areas across the Pacific Ocean, can weigh up to nine pounds (4.1 kg) and have legs up to four feet (1.2 m) long. And don't think you can escape it by staying out of the water—the coconut crab lives most of its life on land. But, as the name suggests, they are nuts for coconuts—not humans!

Despite their large size, however, the crabs can't quite crack the coconuts open. Instead, a coconut crab will climb high in a tree and drop the coconut from there. The coconut is weakened by the fall, and the crab is able to pull the fruit apart with its powerful claws and eat the meat inside. What a *shell*-ebration!

Of course, climbing *up* the tree isn't a problem for the crabs; it's the trip down that doesn't always go so well. Coconut crabs frequently fall out of trees onto unsuspecting people or animals below. Yikes—hope those coconuts are worth it!

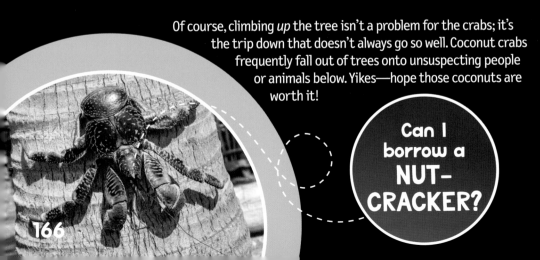

Can I borrow a **NUT-CRACKER?**

They can lift up to **60** pounds (27 kg).

I'm feeling **CRABBY** today!

Coconut crabs will often eat their own **EXOSKELETONS** when they outgrow them.

Signs there's a tiger in your house:

Someone ate all the DELI MEAT.

The couch in the living room is SHREDDED.

Your DOG is hiding under the bed.

The LITTER BOX is overflowing.

That ROARING SOUND isn't your tummy growling.

Dog Eats Diamond

THIS DOG HAS EXPENSIVE TASTE! Soli, a rescued golden retriever, frequently joined his owner George at George's co-owned jewelry store in Maryland, U.S.A. One fateful day, George was examining a three-carat diamond—worth around $20,000 (US$)—when he dropped it on the floor. George searched and searched, but the diamond wasn't anywhere to be found. That's when he realized that Soli must have gobbled it up. George quickly consulted a veterinarian, who advised the dog owner to let nature take its course.

After three tense days of waiting (and lots of walks), Soli ... well ... *returned* the diamond with a plop. The dog was unharmed, George had his inventory back, and the diamond, after a very thorough cleaning, remained intact. What a *ruff* journey!

A vet once reported that he removed **FIVE RUBBER DUCKIES** and a **TOY TRUCK** from a dog's stomach.

All's well that **ENDS** well!

Another dog in Georgia, U.S.A., once ate a packet of diamonds worth **$10,000.**

ANIMAL:

Chinchilla

NAME:

Chris Mass

FAVORITE PASTIME:

Posting elfies

FAVORITE SAYING:

"Never *sleigh* never!"

172

LEMON WAS **NOT** A QUAL-*LEAF*-IED GARDENER.

CRITTER
COMEDIANS
Timon and Pumbaa

WHAT DO YOU GET WHEN YOU CROSS A wisecracking meerkat with a flatulent warthog? Why, the greatest comedy duo of all time!

Timon the merrymaking meerkat and Pumbaa the sweet (but often stinky) warthog are two of the hottest jokesters on the African savanna. They also happen to be great friends of a certain king … lion king, that is. Timon and Pumbaa took a runaway lion cub named Simba under their wing and raised him as part of their grub-eating, singing, worry-free family. And later, they even helped him reclaim his rightful throne.

But enough name-dropping! Whether they're bowling for buzzards, dancing the hula, or juggling plates, these courtly jesters stand out on their own. This wacky pair has appeared in multiple films, in their own TV series, on merchandise, and in theme parks. They never bore their audiences, even the ones that want to eat them. Maybe it's Timon's brash singing voice (think screaming to a melody). Or perhaps it's Pumbaa's clever timing (think screaming swine toots). But this double act is hog wild!

Timon and Pumbaa show Simba, the Lion King, around.

MEERKATS are a type of mongoose.

Warthogs use their **TUSKS** to dig for grubs and insects.

BAFFLING
BATFISH

IF YOU'RE A FISH GETTING READY FOR AN UNDERWATER GALA, what do you wear? Perhaps some festive, bright red lipstick? Don't ask us, ask the batfish!

Found on the bottom of the Pacific Ocean near Cocos Island in Costa Rica, this rare fish looks as if it's wearing glamorous, shocking-red lipstick. While its naturally red lips are (almost certainly) not meant for modeling, scientists aren't quite sure what they are for. Some researchers believe the luscious lips may be a unique way of attracting a mate.

Of course, there's also something even more unusual about the batfish: It can't swim! Yes, you read that right—the batfish can't swim. Instead, it uses its pectoral fins to move across the ocean floor. After all, it already has on glamorous "makeup," so it may as well treat the seabed as a runway!

A batfish's belly is covered in **BONY SCALES.**

I'm a *MODEL* citizen.

A batfish's tail is covered in **LITTLE THORNS.**

ALONSO:
What is a **MONKEY'S** favorite gymnastics move?

LOUISA:
The **SWING?**

ALONSO:
The **BANANA SPLITS.**

180

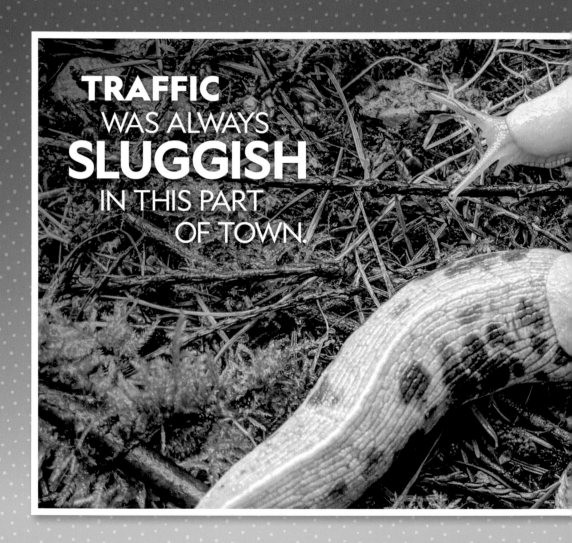

TRAFFIC WAS ALWAYS **SLUGGISH** IN THIS PART OF TOWN.

This is
the last
SLIME
I walk home
this way.

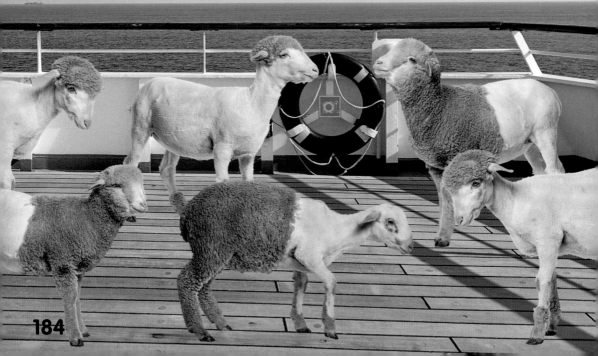

Six shabbily sheared sheep on a ship.

AMUSING ANIMALS

ANIMAL:

Ring-tailed lemur

NAME:

Twister

FAVORITE FOOD:

Pretzels

FAVORITE SAYING:

"*Namaste* in bed today."

I love hanging out here SLOOOOW MUCH!

The snack bandit was a sloth like the one pictured here.

Sloth Snags Snacks

SLOWEST … BREAK-IN … EVER. In what was possibly the cutest robbery of all time, a café in Costa Rica became the victim of a furry intruder who tripped the burglar alarm. A sloth snuck into the café after closing time and was captured on video climbing slowly and steadily along the counter, searching for a delicious stash of nighttime snacks. As the slow-moving intruder was investigating the counter area, he lost his balance and fell, hitting the ground with a thump. Unharmed, he continued his search— unaware that the noise had triggered the alarm.

Alerted to a possible break-in, the owners hastily dashed to the café. When they arrived, they were shocked to find the culprit was a hungry sloth! The owners managed to move the sluggish rascal back to his tree. They later said that their café is no stranger to four-legged customers. They are frequently visited by monkeys and toucans (who never tip), but this was their first sloth. So what made him visit? Perhaps this slowpoke just wanted to hang out at the café, or maybe he needed a cup of *sloth-ee* to get moving.

Sloths are **GREAT** swimmers.

Sloths only come down from trees **ONCE A WEEK** to go to the bathroom.

187

The cat catchers can't catch caught cats.

BAD KITTY

188

Whew! So glad to be out. There was **NO WI-FI** in there.

CRITTER COMEDIANS

Tuna Melts My Heart

BEAUTY COMES IN ALL SHAPES AND SIZES. Just ask Tuna, a dachshund/Chihuahua mix and proud bearer of big ears, a wrinkly neck, and a giant overbite. This combination of odd features might sound wacky, but it's a recipe for adorable. Don't believe it? Just ask any one of Tuna's almost two million social media followers.

At four months old, Tuna was abandoned on the side of a California, U.S.A., road. Luckily, he was rescued and put up for adoption. Because Tuna has a unique appearance, people were worried he might not find a home. But when Courtney Dasher saw the little guy, she immediately fell in love! Courtney realized that Tuna had something special and wanted to share his cute face and unique outlook on life with the world. That's when Tuna unleashed his star power. He quickly became an internet sensation. He also *paw*-thored a book and has roamed the world promoting it.

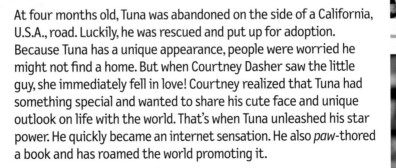

On top of that, Tuna and his human use his fame to raise awareness and money for animal rescues. Tuna's physical differences and fetching outfits have only helped spread the message that beauty comes from within.

"CHIWEENIE" is a cute term for a dachshund/Chihuahua mix.

Tuna has made numerous TV appearances.

Tuna's original name was **WORMY** because he crawled around on his belly.

Next time I'll pony up for airline tickets.

THE KITTEN THOUGHT HER **TAXI RIDE** WAS A **NIGHT-MARE.**

OWL
be keeping
my eye
on you.

LAUGHING RATS

HA! HA! HA! HA! HA!

HA–HA! STOP! I can't take it! You're hilarious!

SCIENCE IS ALWAYS SURPRISING US with exciting and groundbreaking discoveries. But the cutest discovery ever made? Probably when scientists learned that rats can laugh!

And just how did scientists learn this? Well, by tickling rats, of course. Picture it: Leading scientists at Humboldt University in Germany gathered around a rat, "coochi-coo-ing" the rodent and recording the results. OK, so it was way more technical than that, but the results are still *rat*-astic. The scientists used electrodes to harmlessly tickle the rats' tummies, backs, and tails—and the rats let out squeaks of glee! Actually, the squeaks themselves were too high-pitched to be heard by the human ear. But when the recordings were slowed down, the scientists heard rat laughter!

Now that's something to giggle about!

DOGS have their own form of laughing, but it is more of a pant.

The study of laughter and its effects on the body is called **GELOTOLOGY.**

195

CRITTER COMEDIANS
Daffy Duck

HE SINGS, HE DANCES, HE ACTS, BUT HE NEVER QUACKS ... despite the fact he's a duck. Even so, Daffy Duck certainly makes others *quack* up! He just doesn't know he's doing it.

For more than 80 years, Daffy has been making audiences laugh with his explosive personality, wise-guy wit, and unpredictable antics. In fact, he's so popular that he's appeared in television shows, films, and comics, and also has his own merchandise. Of course, Daffy doesn't always realize when he's being hilarious! The delightful duck is determined to be a star, but due to his short temper and rather large ego, Daffy often finds himself in a host of misadventures, from fighting with Elmer Fudd to piano duels to going undercover as a detective.

And, of course, Daffy's rivalry with Bugs Bunny doesn't help things! Determined to be the center of attention, Daffy will do anything to steal the spotlight. Unfortunately for him, Bugs always seems to have the upper hand. But that's OK—as long as Daffy keeps trying, audiences are sure to keep laughing!

Holidays at the farm:

MEW YEAR'S DAY

APRIL FOALS' DAY

HOWL-OWEEN

ST. RAT-RICK'S DAY

INDE-HEN-DENCE DAY

Stay
COO
until next
time!

CREDITS

Abbreviations: AL = Alamy Stock Photo; DRMS = Dreamstime; GI = Getty Images; IS = iStockphoto; MP = Minden Pictures; RF = Rex Features; SS = Shutterstock

Cover (orangutans), DLILLC/Corbis/VCG/GI; (dog), Grigorita Ko/SS; back cover (LE), Capuski/GI; (LE, costume), AlohaHawaii/SS; (RT), Buy This/SS; spine (llama) hjochen/SS; (microphone) Maksym Bondarchuk/SS; (sunglasses) visivastudio/SS; (hat) homydesign/SS; (chains) Reamolko/SS;1, James Brey/GI; 2 (disco ball), Oxy_gen/SS; (dog) Javier Brosch/SS; (llama), Hjochen/SS; (microphone), Maksym Bondarchuk/SS; (sunglasses), Visiva Studio/SS; (hat), Homy Design/SS; (necklace), Reamolko/SS; (chicken), Shevs/SS; 3 (candles), Brad Calkins/DRMS; (cake), Pongphan Ruengchai/DRMS; (party hat), Alexandr Zagibalov/SS; (toucans), Edurivero/DRMS; 4, Arif Supriyadi/SS; 5 (dog), J Staley 401/SS; (shoes), Africa Studio/SS; 6, Rovio/Columbia/Sony Animation/Village Roadshow/Kobal/SS; 7, Rovio/Columbia/Sony Animation/Village Roadshow/Kobal/SS; 8, Aydin Mutlu/GI; 9 (chameleon), Kuttelvaserova Stuchelova/SS; (black hat), Ljupco Smokovski/SS; (crocodile), Dang Dumrong/SS; (money bag), Ned Napa/SS; (bracelet), Stock Shoppe/SS; 10 (cows), Colombo Nicola/SS; (necklace), Karen Barrett York/SS; 12 (back), Megan Lorenz/GI; 13 (hard hat), Eranicle/SS; Eric Isselee/SS; (truck), Phat1978/SS; 14 (dog), Annette Shaff/SS; (scarf), Jac_cz/SS; 15 (goggles), Arty U Studio/SS; 16 (chicken), Shevs/SS; (back), Front Page/SS; 17, Shikheigoh/GI; 18 (top hat), Bale Fire/SS; 19 (mouse toy), Yellow Cat/SS; (cat), Eric Isselee/DRMS; (necklace), Mcmc/SS; (pendant), Mega Pixel/SS; (money), Lifetime Stock/SS; (jewels), Tara Patta/SS; (bowl), Lyubov Nazarova/SS; 20 (dog), J Staley 401/SS; 21 (back), Lukasz Janyst/DRMS; (hat) Zim235/DRMS; (camel), Marifa/DRMS; 22-23, Courtesy of Venusmom; 23 (hearts), Premium Vector/SS; 24, Birkir Asgeirsson/SS; 25 (brown stick bug), Cyno Club/SS; (stick bug close-up), Petr Lerch/SS; (stick bug side view), Eric Isselee/SS; (green stick bugs), Cristina Romero Palma/SS; (ice pack), Birgit Reitz-Hofmann/SS; (thermometer), Francticoo0/SS; (tissue box), Stuar/SS; 26, Oxygen/SS; 27 (peacock spider), Bios Photo/AL; (dancefloor), Vector Plus/SS; 28 (cat), Mriya Wildlife/SS; 29 (cow), Dudarev Mikhail/SS; (brown cow), Kurt/SS; (3D glasses), Sergey Mironov/SS; (popcorn), M. Unal Ozmen/SS; (soda), Anton Starikov/SS; 30 (giraffe front view), Helo80808/DRMS; (ostrich close-up), Komilov Dream/DRMS; (hat), Yuki Hipo/SS; (giraffe side), Elgreko/SS; (ostrich side), Zhanna Prokopeva/SS; (ostrich open mouth), Nadiya Vlashchenko/DRMS; 31, Abeselom Zerit/SS; 32, Katho Menden/SS; 33 (chef hat), Photo Melon/SS; (polar bear), Volkova Natalia/SS; (spoon), Yingko/SS; (napkin), NYS/SS; (pot) S Photo/SS; 34 (back), Dudarev Mikhail/SS; 35, Lauren Skeoch and Den Yoga NOTL; 36 (cat), Ingret/SS; 37 (back), Debu55y/DRMS; (mouse), James Brey/GI; 38 (Christmas lights), Eklèr/SS; (brown

Christmas tree worm), Jon Milnes/SS; 39 (blue Christmas tree worm), J'nel/SS; (ornaments), Graphix Mania/SS; (gifts), Ecco/SS; 40, Shippee/DRMS; 41, Grigorita Ko/SS; 42, Shirley Nordenskiold/@exoticherman/RF; 43 (cat close up), Shirley Nordenskiold/@exoticherman/RF; (cat lying down), Barcroft Media/GI; (elf cat), Barcroft Media/GI; (cat with toy), Barcroft Media/GI; (cat in basket), Barcroft Media/GI; 44, Agus Fitriyanto Suratno/SS; 45, Vladimir Melnik/SS; (binoculars), Draft Mode/DRMS; (book), Fototo Cam/DRMS; 46 (popcorn), Ilya Akinshin/SS; (guinea pig), Juniors Bildarchiv GmbH/AL; (popcorn pile) Urfin/SS; 48, Vicnt/GI; 49 (fireworks), Andrii_M/SS; (baboon), Patrice Correia/DRMS; (baboon sitting), Eric Isselee/SS; (firecrackers), Patryk Kosmider/SS; 50, Everett Collection Inc./AL; 51 (fox and rabbit), Moviestore/SS; 52 (back), Arina P Habich/SS; (dog) JLfotoNL/SS; 53 (back), World Wide/SS; (fawn), Eric Isselee/SS; 54, Best Dog Photo/SS; 56 (back), Suti Stock Photo/SS; (Santa hat) Photo Pixel/SS; (snakes) Werg/SS; 57 (sheep), Capuski/GI; (chicken hat), Aloha Hawaii/SS; 58 (police lights), Kindlena/SS; (horse), Courtesy of Sandra Boos; 59 (horse with flowers), Courtesy of Sandra Boos; 60 (back), Cara-Foto/SS; (umbrella), Tatiana Popova/SS; (weasel arched back), GlobalP/GI; (weasel), Eric Isselee/SS; (hat), Nerthuz/SS; 61 Mike Raabe/GI; 62 (dog close-up), Broadimage/SS; (dog with bandana), Solar/Ave Pictures/SS; (dog in costume), Eric Charbonneau/SS; (dog in purse), Emma McIntyre/KCS2018/GI; (dog in shirt), Broadimage/SS; 63, Justin Sullivan/GI; 64, Godi Photo/SS; 65 (back), FCA Foto Digital/GI; 65 (cat) Kuban Girl/DRMS; (hot sauce), Travis Manley/DRMS; 66 (hat), Pix Fiction/SS; 67 (library), Huating/DRMS; (crow), Eric Isselee/DRMS; (books), Maskarad/DRMS; 68 (back), Baloncici/GI; (broccoli), Nik Merkulov/SS; (cat), Zanna Pesnina/SS; 69 (turtles), Thomas Pajot/SS; (ball), Chernetskaya/DRMS; 70, Outcast85/SS; 71 (cough medicine), Africa Studio/SS; (tissue), Kaiskynet Studio/SS; (tissue box), Kaiskynet Studio/SS; 72 (back), Gwoeii/SS; (ferrets), Eric Isselee/SS; 73 4FR/GI; 74, Images by Brooke/GI; 76 (theater), Ket4up/SS; (elephants), Givaga/SS; (tiger), Atiger/SS; (deer), Nickolay Stanev/SS; (zebra), Amber Earnest/SS; 77, Buy This/SS; 78 (whale), Wildest Animal/SS; 79 (toilet paper), Suprunvitaly/DRMS; (ambergris), Alex Farias/SS; 80, Vladimir Wrangel/SS; 81 (llama), Hjochen/SS; (microphone), Maksym Bondarchuk/SS; (sunglasses), Visiva Studio/SS; (hat) Homy Design/SS; (necklace), Reamolko/SS; (dog) Javier Brosch/SS; 82, Magalie St-Hilaire Poulin/SS; 84 (back), Maria Skaldina/SS; (dog), Posh Portraits/GI; 85, Grigorita Ko/SS; 86-87, Courtesy of Stacy Daniels; 88, Kurit Afshen/SS; 89, Mr. Rizz Business; 90, John Shearer/GI; 91 (pug close-up), Eye DJ/SS; (dog in king costume), Ken McKay/ITV/SS; (dog in tuxedo costume) Lev Radin/SS; (dog with book), Paul Brown/SS; (dog in jean vest), Debby Wong/SS; (dog in yellow scarf), Paul Brown/SS; 92, Mike Korostelev/SS; 93 (back), Didecs/DRMS; (chick), Urosh Petrovic/GI; 94, Izanbar/

COPYRIGHT

Since 1888, the National Geographic Society has funded more than 12,000 research, exploration, and preservation projects around the world. The Society receives funds from National Geographic Partners, LLC, funded in part by your purchase. A portion of the proceeds from this book supports this vital work. To learn more, visit natgeo.com/info.

For more information, visit nationalgeographic.com, call 1-877-873-6846, or write to the following address:

National Geographic Partners
1145 17th Street N.W.
Washington, DC 20036-4688 U.S.A.

Visit us online at nationalgeographic.com/books

For librarians and teachers: nationalgeographic.com/books/librarians-and-educators

More for kids from National Geographic: natgeokids.com

National Geographic Kids magazine inspires children to explore their world with fun yet educational articles on animals, science, nature, and more. Using fresh storytelling and amazing photography, *Nat Geo Kids* shows kids ages 6 to 14 the fascinating truth about the world—and why they should care. **kids.nationalgeographic.com/subscribe**

For rights or permissions inquiries, please contact National Geographic Books Subsidiary Rights: bookrights@natgeo.com

Designed by Rosie Gowsell Pattison

Trade paperback ISBN: 978-1-4263-3687-4
Reinforced library binding ISBN: 978-1-4263-3688-1

The publisher would like to thank Plan B Book Packagers, author; Paige Towler, project editor; Lori Epstein, photo director; Joan Gossett, production editor; and Anne LeongSon and Gus Tello, production assistants.

Printed in Hong Kong
20/PPHK/1